CREATING YOUR
success
PLAN

A CAREER SUCCESS GUIDE FOR WOMEN

JANICE L. LAMY

Creating Your Success Plan: A Career Success Guide for Women

Copyright © 2019 Janice L Lamy

All rights reserved. No part of this book may be reproduced or transmitted in any form or by any means, electronic or mechanical, including photocopying, recording or by any information storage and retrieval system, without written permission from the author, except for the inclusion of brief quotations in a review.

The advice and strategies found in this book may not be suitable for every situation. This work is sold with the understanding that neither the author nor the publisher is held responsible for the results accrued from the advice in this book.

Cover Design by 100Covers.com
Interior Design by FormattedBooks.com

ISBN 978-0-587-54146-4

CHECK OUT THE SUCCESS PLAN COURSE AVAILABLE AT

www.CreatingYourSuccessPlan.com

••

The Success Plan Course makes it easy to navigate the process of creating your plan. It includes video tutorials and guidance, along with resources you will find helpful in completing your plan quickly and effectively!

THANK YOU!

• •

As a thanks for buying my book and taking an amazing first step toward your future career success, I would like to offer you a discounted membership in the Success Plan Community where you'll meet like-minded women who are focused on their futures, find resources to help keep you motivated, and more!

Simply go to

www.creatingyoursuccessplan.com/communityoffer

Looking forward to seeing you there!

TABLE OF CONTENTS

Introduction XI

    My Intention for You. XI
    How This Book Is Organized XIII

Section 1: Creating Your Success Plan. 1

    Chapter 1: Your Core Values and Focus Statement . . . 3
        Your Core Values. 4
        Your Focus Statement 10
        Optional: Your Supporting Behaviors. 12

    Chapter 2: Your Success Plan. 15
        Obstacles You May Face: Fears, Limiting
        Beliefs, and the Myth of Perfection 16
        The 3-, 5-, and 10-Year Framework. 17
        Step 1: Your 10-Year Goals 18
        Step 2: Your 5-Year Goals 22

Step 3: Your 3-Year Goals .25
Step 4: Your Milestones to Success 27

Chapter 3: Your Marketing Plan 31
Part 1: Your Professional Brand Statement and Promise. 32
Part 2: Your Positioning Objectives. 35
Part 3: Your Target Audiences 36
Part 4: Your Tactics. 38
Part 5: Measurement and Tracking. 43

Chapter 4: Visualizing Success and Giving Up "The How" 46
Your Visualization Process 47
Giving up "The How" 49

Section 2: Guidance for Success 53

Success Tip 1: Attracting Success—The Law of Attraction 55
Attracting Success Through Gratitude 58
Attracting Success by Creating the Culture You Want (Even If It's a Micro-Culture) 62

Success Tip 2: Learning for Success—Invest in Yourself 66
Decision Point: Advanced Degree?. 68
More Tips on Learning. .70

Success Tip 3: Networking for Success 73
Setting Up Your Network 74

Additional Networking Tips................77

Success Tip 4: Balancing for Success 79
    Balancing Point: Motherhood.................79

Success Tip 5: Shifting for Success 83
    Learning 84
    Managing 84
    Leading................................85
    Mentoring 86

Wrapping It All Up: Get Ready to Succeed!.......91

Acknowledgments.............................95

About the Author............................97

INTRODUCTION

My Intention for You

Congratulations on taking an amazing first step toward creating a meaningful, successful career! I am so pleased to provide guidance and mentorship to you through this book. What you will discover and experience as you work through the steps I have laid out will be foundational to your current and ongoing success.

I created this book to help women in the early- and mid-stages of their careers navigate their professional lives as effectively as possible. I did not have this kind of resource available during those phases of my career, and I never identified a mentor to help guide me along the way. Looking back, I would have been more successful, faster, if I had a Success Plan to guide me. If I had taken the time to identify my core values, think through what success meant to me, and find a mentor or a community for exchanging ideas, not only would I have avoided a few not-so-great career moves, I would have achieved more in much less time.

It seems like common sense to me now, but without having this kind of support and guidance in place, I simply navigated blindly through my thirty-plus-year career. That's not to say I'm not proud of what I've achieved—quite the contrary. I've done some amazing things in my career and have had opportunities to work with incredible people and forward-thinking organizations. But my experience could have been much richer and even more rewarding if I had my own Success Plan to follow, helping chart my course to professional fulfillment.

This book is designed specifically for women because, let's face it, we are different from men. We approach our work from a unique perspective—one that values collaboration, nurturing, relationships, and communication. Men, on the other hand, focus more on a linear course to advancement. They have typically been conditioned to be the main breadwinner of the family and are usually laser-focused and intent on success. Women can find it more difficult to focus as intently on their professional lives, given the additional responsibilities that come with children and taking care of aging parents.

I acknowledge that these statements are generalities and there are definitely exceptions to these career approaches in both genders. However, for the most part, men and women are different in the way they think about and approach their careers. There's a reason the book *Men Are From Mars, Women Are From Venus,* by John Gray, was such a huge success—it helped us understand and appreciate our differences.

Perhaps partly due to these differences, gender disparities in leadership roles continue to be significant. This is evidenced in a 2018 study conducted by LeanIn.Org and McKinsey & Company titled *Women in the Workplace*. It is the largest comprehensive study of the state of women in corporate America and has been conducted annually since 2015. The 2018 study points out that "for the last four years, companies have reported that they are highly committed to gender diversity. But that commitment has not translated into meaningful progress. The proportion of women at every level in corporate America has hardly changed. Progress isn't just slow. It's stalled."

My hope is that, by focusing on helping women create their career Success Plans, together we can play a role in addressing these disparities and moving forward in a positive, proactive manner. It's the kind of progress that is made one by one, and we need to do what we can to make it happen. By taking the time to intentionally think through what you want to achieve in your career, no matter how intangible and distant it might feel, you can set the course for a very rewarding professional life. That is my intention for you.

How This Book Is Organized

There are two sections in this book. The first is all about creating your Success Plan. As you read through this section you will learn about key factors that will drive your Success Plan. Don't forget to check out the Success Plan Course that can be found at www.CreatingYourSuccessPlan.com. The Course provides additional guidance and video tutorials to help you create your Success Plan.

First, you will identify your core values and create a personal focus statement. You'll single out what matters most to you with regard to your professional life—something very few people ever take the time to do. These tools will help you make decisions as you navigate your career.

Then, you will use this base to create your Success Plan, which will encompass 3, 5, and 10-year goals for your career with in-depth visualizations of what success looks and feels like along the way. This process may be quite easy for some, but for most of us, it takes a lot of thought, guidance, and introspection. You may not have all the answers immediately, and that's fine. The more you work at this and invest time in planning for your future, the clearer everything will become.

The last component of your Success Plan is your marketing plan. Yes, you must market yourself in order to be successful and achieve your goals more quickly! I include guidance on how to develop your personal brand and market yourself, each and every day—because each day you are actually interviewing for your next opportunity! Self-promotion, based on the goals you have identified in your Success Plan, is an important key to your ultimate success and it's something women usually avoid.

I know this sounds like a *lot* right now, but you can do it. And you will enjoy the process!

The second section is devoted to providing tips and guidance as you work toward fulfilling your Success Plan. These Success Tips include how to attract success into your life by living according to the Law of Attraction, how to continually learn and listen in order to succeed, and how to network effectively. The Law of Attraction simply states that what you think about becomes your reality. You can, therefore, create whatever you want in your career by setting clear goals and visualizing how success looks and feels and remaining focused on it, which is the foundation of your Success Plan!

I cannot overstate the importance of continual learning. You make yourself more valuable by mastering and applying new skills. If you choose not to do this, not only do you become stagnant, but you actually decrease your value over time. You'll be left in the dust of your colleagues who are proactively growing and learning!

You can continually learn from multiple avenues. One such avenue is through your network. Networking is an essential skill that I did not fully appreciate until later in my career. It takes time and intentional nurturing to build your network of contacts and mentors, as well as those you mentor. By starting a focused networking program early in your career, you will create a circle of valuable resources and reach your goals much faster and with less effort.

Additionally, I cover the importance of balancing your life effectively. As women, we need to consider whether motherhood is in our future, and if so, how we will accommodate that important life stage in our Success Plan. It's important to understand that we cannot perform every aspect of our life at 100 percent all the time. We must mindfully choose to focus on what matters most at present.

Next, I have included Success Tips on "shifting"—realizing that we shift our focus roughly each decade of our career, from learning to managing, then leading and ultimately mentoring. I provide guidance on how to leverage each phase to your best advantage.

Throughout this section, I have incorporated real-life examples from my experiences as well as those of women I have had the honor of working with and learning from over the course of the past thirty years. These examples should help bring the concepts to life and provide inspiration for you.

The last chapter is designed to help launch your Success Plan and provide guidance on how to remain focused. It is vital to keep your Plan top of mind and refreshed on an ongoing basis. Now, let's get started!

SECTION 1: CREATING YOUR SUCCESS PLAN

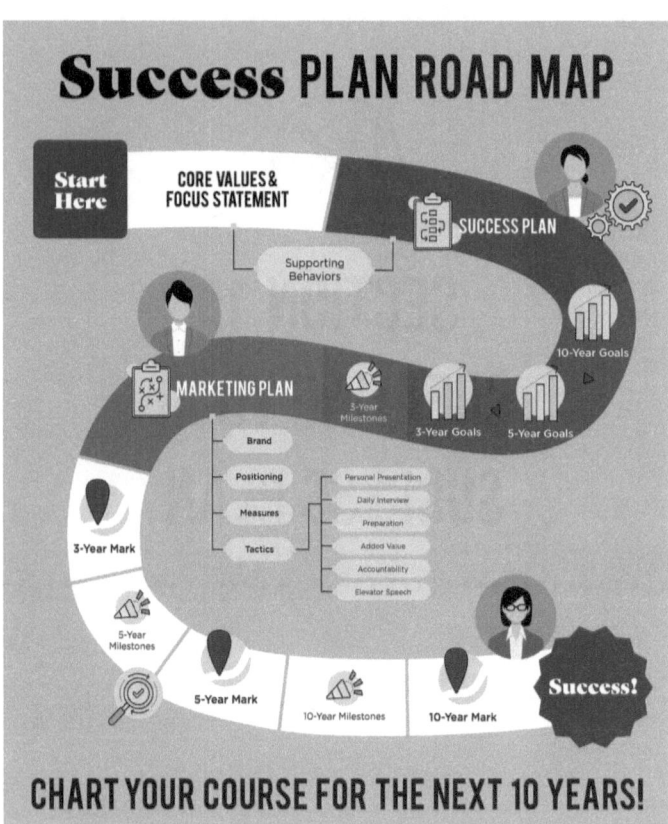

CHAPTER 1:
YOUR CORE VALUES AND FOCUS STATEMENT

Most organizations have a list of core values and a mission statement that employees should know, internalize (or at least memorize), and follow. Since these tools can guide their decisions and set the course for the organization's success, leaders spend a lot of intentional thought on creating them, communicating them, and keeping them relevant.

So too, your core values and subsequent focus statement are the guideposts for creating your Success Plan. Identifying your core values is foundational to being truly clear on what you want to manifest and achieve in your career. Unfortunately, so many of us never take the time to establish them for ourselves. It just never occurs to us. As a matter of fact, I hadn't considered doing so until later in my career—and I can tell you that going through the process gave me more focus than I've ever had in my life. By doing this earlier in your career, you will give yourself an amazing advantage and a springboard to success.

Your Core Values

Defining your core values helps you understand what is important to you, and why. It's like setting up your own internal navigation system to guide you in creating your Success Plan. Writing your focus statement, based upon your core values, helps define the purpose and direction for your career. Without these tools in place, you are basically moving through life in a fog and probably following someone else's purpose rather than your own!

So to start, create a list of the things you find important in life, specifically as they relate to your career. This list might come easily to you, or it could be a bit challenging. If you're having trouble getting started, search terms like "values" and "career values" online to find some inspiration. If you opted to enroll in the Success Plan Course, you have access to a list of potential values for you to review and consider, as well as virtual worksheets to help guide you.

Take some time with this—don't be tempted to rush through the process. Make a list of 10–15 values that resonate with you. If you feel comfortable, share your list with a family member or friend to get their input. Ask them questions including:

- Does the list seem to match up with what you know about me?

- Which ones seem the most like me?

- Can you suggest other values to consider?

This is a great opportunity to learn about yourself and possibly identify something that you didn't know is important to you. Again, take your time, and be comforted knowing that you have the inner wisdom to do this—it's all right there inside.

Once you have your list of values, sort through them and determine which ones really stand out to you. Work toward getting the list narrowed down to five core values. Some of them will naturally combine into one; others will be unique. Once you've done this, you might want to put the list aside and come back to it later—perhaps sleep on it overnight and then review the list of five once more. Take time to make adjustments if needed.

Now, here's the fun part: prioritize them in order of importance! Yes, each one must be ranked from one to five, with one being the most important. You may find this difficult to do, but it is essential to your success. Ranking your values can make a big difference in how you set up your Success Plan and what you focus on most.

Here's an example to help illustrate this point. Imagine that two people, Jane and Tricia, come up with the exact same list of five core values. Chances are they would rank them differently, which will mean they approach their careers differently.

Set of Core Values Identified by Jane and Tricia:

Achievement, Recognition, Growth, Finances, Excitement

Jane's prioritized list:

Finances, Growth, Achievement, Recognition, Excitement

Tricia's prioritized list:

Excitement, Achievement, Growth, Recognition, Finances

Both Jane and Tricia have the same list of values, but they prioritized them very differently. Where Jane would be very focused on her salary and growing her career, Tricia would opt for more focus on having fun in her career with less importance on her salary. Thus, these two women would likely take dramatically different career paths—both ultimately being successful and happy, but by different metrics of success. Given this example, you can see why you need to rank your core values.

Ranking your values can be a challenge. If you hit a roadblock, talk with someone who knows you well and can help you prioritize your values. Take time to reflect on their feedback. You might agree with them, or you might not. Either way, this could help clarify things for you.

A fun way to approach this is to write each value on a separate small piece of paper, fold each one up, and put them in a container. Then, pull one out and consider it as your number one core value. If it is, great; if not, pull another one until you feel confident in your selection. Then repeat this process as needed until you have them ranked in an order that works for you.

Once you have your final set of core values ranked in order of importance, list them out and add a definition for each, written in present tense as though you are living this core value today. In your own words, write what you believe they mean to you. Don't use the exact definition you find when you search the word online, but instead use that as a starting point if needed. Your definition will likely be different from the way anyone else would define the same value.

Consider how Jane's and Tricia's core value definitions might differ:

Jane's core values and their definitions:

Finances

> I am focused on aggressively growing my income to keep pace with my career achievements. I save an appropriate amount each month to support reaching my goals to invest and buy a home.

Growth

> I look for opportunities to learn and grow in my career, and as such, I am seen as a rising star in my place of work. I regularly reflect on where I am going in my career.

Achievement

> I enjoy achieving my goals and objectives. Once I accomplish something, I immediately set forth toward my next goal or objective.

Recognition

> I appreciate bring recognized for the work that I do. I regularly report key metrics to leaders to keep them updated and aware.

Excitement

> I enjoy the excitement of achieving my goals and objectives, and I get a lot of personal fulfillment from my work.

Tricia's core values and their definitions:

Excitement

I love making a difference in other people's lives. My work is fun and exciting and ever-changing—no two days are ever alike!

Achievement

I celebrate my achievements by doing something fun with friends; life is a continual celebration for me.

Growth

I enjoy learning and growing in every aspect of my life; as I learn more, I am able to help more people.

Recognition

I love to share recognition with others. Everything we do requires teamwork, and I value celebrating successes as a team.

Finances

I appreciate the income I make from doing work that I love. I invest in myself and give to charities that align with my values.

Wow! Two very different approaches to defining their core values, right? Give yourself creative license to define your values in a way that works best for you. This is something you will refer to frequently, so make sure they each really resonate with you.

Once you have your core values defined, take a moment to celebrate what you just accomplished! You have identified, ranked, and personally defined your core values for your career. This is something very few people take the time to do, and it is so important for your success. And it feels good, doesn't it?

Personal Example: My Core Values and Their Definitions

As I went through this process, I learned a lot about what matters most to me at this point in my life. It was difficult to narrow my list down to five, but it was well worth the effort. Notice that my definitions are very personal and not what you might find in a dictionary.

Authentic

> *I am true to myself and therefore others; having the courage to show up and allow myself to be open, honest, and real in all instances; listening to others and helping them live an authentic life, as well.*

Mindful

> *I pay attention on purpose, in the present moment, and nonjudgmentally—creating space for catching insights and making choices based upon my chosen values.*

Grateful

> *I take time each day to recognize and be grateful for the spiritual, material, and relationship gifts I have. When difficult situations arise, I am grateful for them and look deeply to learn the lessons they are offering.*

Responsible

> *I accept responsibility for everything that happens in my life, the way I respond, the way I engage in life, my successes, achievements, and learning experiences.*

Wholehearted

> *I am fully engaged in life, cultivating the courage, compassion, and connection to be present each day and take note of the extraordinary things that occur. I step up and connect with others in order to grow individually while supporting them to live wholeheartedly.*

Your Focus Statement

Next, let's create your focus statement. Here, you will write one or two present tense sentences that connect each of your five core values, in order of importance. The purpose of this task is to create a concise statement that is easy to remember and helps keep you focused on what is important to you with regard to your career and Success Plan. Let's look at a couple of examples, based on Jane's and Tricia's five core values from the last section:

Jane's core values:

Finances, Growth, Achievement, Recognition, Excitement

Jane's focus statement:

My career path provides ample opportunities for increasing my salary and growing professionally. I am able to achieve great results and receive the recognition I deserve, which is exciting for me.

Tricia's core values:

Excitement, Achievement, Growth, Recognition, Finances

Tricia's focus statement:

I have chosen a career that offers excitement and the opportunity to achieve amazing things. There are plenty of opportunities for growth and recognition, and I am able to live comfortably.

Combining your core values into a concise statement can really help bring them to life! You will find a worksheet to help with this in the Success Plan Course that accompanies this book. Take your time with this and make it feel real for you.

Once you've completed this exercise, take time to reflect on how you can use your new core values and focus statement to make important decisions about your career. Can you see how they can help guide you on making your next career move? Have you uncovered new insights into what's important to you professionally? This can be a very empowering process to complete.

Optional: Your Supporting Behaviors

Consider creating a list of supporting behaviors to accompany your core values and focus statement. When I went through this process and narrowed my list of values down to five, I realized that some of the remaining values I had listed were also really important to me, so I didn't want to let them go. However, I knew I had to keep my core values to a manageable number.

So, I chose to add them as behaviors that supported my core values and focus statement. Again, as I did with my core values, I added a present tense definition to each of the supporting behaviors and made sure to link them to one or more of my values. Supporting behaviors can help serve as a guide for how you approach your professional life and add more dimension to your core values.

> **Personal Example:**
> **My Supporting Behaviors and Their Definitions**

To help illustrate how this works, here's my list of supporting behaviors and the definitions I created for each of them. As I thought about it, I realized how each one could support one or more of my core values.

> ***Balance*** *– I am mindful to maintain a good balance between my work and personal life in support of my values to live authentically and wholeheartedly.*
>
> ***Creativity*** *– I honor and support creativity in all endeavors, taking time to connect with my creative nature when engaging in life.*
>
> ***Optimism*** *– I remain positive and expect the best from life; refrain from becoming negative; find the positive aspect of all situations.*
>
> ***Connectedness*** *– I realize and appreciate the connection between all people and nature; use this connection to live life more fully.*
>
> ***Wellness*** *– I engage in healthy living on a daily basis, incorporating movement and self-care along with healthy foods in support of overall well-being.*

You can see how these behaviors help me live according to my core values. If the process of identifying supporting behaviors serves you and seems like a good idea, go ahead and add them.

Going forward, you will want to keep your core values and focus statement nearby and easily accessible (along with the supporting behaviors if you choose to add them). Put them into your notes app on your smartphone, print them and keep them in your handbag, or tape them onto your bathroom mirror—or all of the above! You will need to review them frequently to keep them top of mind so you can remain focused.

Once you have completed identifying your core values, created your focus statement, and potentially added some supporting behaviors, you can begin working on your Success Plan. You'll begin thinking about what you want to achieve over the next ten years and setting specific goals to get there. This will be hard work, but definitely worth every second you spend on it. Time to take on chapter two!

CHAPTER 2: YOUR SUCCESS PLAN

Now that you have your foundation in place—your core values, focus statement, and optional supporting behaviors—it's time to create your Success Plan. This can also be one of the most useful and rewarding experiences of your life, but it is also a place where many people get stuck.

Obstacles You May Face: Fears, Limiting Beliefs, and the Myth of Perfection

One of the primary reasons this process can be difficult is fear. The fear of failure, to be specific. This fear can take many forms: doubting your ability to create a good Success Plan; fearing failure in your attempts to create one; worrying that after you spend a lot of time creating your Plan, you will not be able to make it happen; fearing criticism from others or the possibility that you will encounter obstacles along the way that will cause you to fail.

Sometimes these fears stem from limiting beliefs. Somewhere deep down you might think you don't deserve success. You might have seen a parent or other important person in your life struggle to succeed and subconsciously believe success just isn't in the cards for you. It's amazing how negative experiences from early in our lives can have a lasting impact if we allow them to—don't let this happen to you!

Additionally, don't get too hung up on the myth of perfection and creating the perfect plan. Rest assured it will more than likely change over the course of the next 10 years, and that's OK. Things will happen in your chosen industry, disruptive new technologies might shift your focus, and you could even find a completely new career path that interests you. Life is ever-changing, and so are you. Just focus on creating the Plan that works for you, right where you are today. And allow yourself permission to revise it as needed.

It's completely normal to find this work challenging and a bit frightening. After all, it's really important work and takes a lot of time, energy, and personal reflection. But you owe it to yourself to push past any fears, doubts, limiting beliefs, and the need to be perfect. Your future success depends upon your ability to move forward and create your Plan. You really do deserve it!

The 3-, 5-, and 10-Year Framework

You will divide your Success Plan into three sections: a set of goals to reach in three years, another set in five years, and ultimately goals that will bring you to where you want to be in ten years. As a living, breathing document, you will continually update your plan with each career move and as you achieve your goals along the way. It is never truly final—until, of course, you reach all of your goals!

The best way to get started on your Success Plan is to start at the end and work your way back to the beginning. By that, I mean start with your 10-year goals, then set your 5-year goals based on being halfway there, and lastly your 3-year goals to establish the foundation of your success path.

The Importance of Visualization and Giving Up "The How"

One of the most important parts of this process is visualization. As you set your goals, you will visualize how it will look and feel to achieve them. The more detailed your visualizations, the better. We will walk through how to do that once you have your goals identified. Keep this in mind as you write your goals—include details that bring your goals to life and make it easy to visualize achieving them. This can be a lot of fun—let your creativity flow as you picture yourself succeeding at each phase of your career!

Allow yourself to set aggressive, lofty goals without worrying about how you will achieve them. As you work through achieving your Success Plan over the next 10 years, you will learn that "the how" will come to you when the time is right. All you have to do is set your goals, visualize success with detail and feeling, and never give up. Be sure to aim high with your goals and believe you can achieve them. And you will. OK, let's get started!

Step 1: Your 10-Year Goals

The first step in creating your 10-year goals is to identify where you aspire to be 10 years from today. I refer to this as your 10-year aspirations. Get started by making sure you are in a comfortable place with no distractions and ask yourself a few questions, like those listed below, to get your creative thoughts flowing. There is a section in the Success Plan Course to help you with this process.

Questions to Help Identify Your 10-year Aspirations

- Where do you want to be in 10 years? (Note: Don't let this one intimidate you; take a deep breath and really let yourself have fun with this!)

- What stage of your career are you in—contributing as an individual, managing, or leading?

- What types of responsibilities do you have?

- Do you work in an office setting or somewhere else? What does your workplace look like?

- What does it feel like to have achieved this level of success?

- How have things changed in your personal life because of your success?

- What is your financial situation like?

- How are your living your core values?

Keep working at this until you have a clear picture, or vision, of where you are and what you are doing in 10 years. Take as much time as you need. Have fun with it!

It's often helpful to find one or more people who are currently in the role you aspire to—let's call them role models—and learn about them. Identify one to three role models by conducting research into how they achieved success. What you learn may provide inspiration for setting your goals across the 10-year period of your Success Plan.

Use the following questions as a guide for your research. Find the answers by speaking directly with your role model or others who know her, searching online, or combining these methods.

Prompts for Your Role Model Research

- What makes them successful?

- How did they get there? What were their career paths?

- Are any of them mentor material?

- Could you reach out and make them part of your network?

- Who is in their network?

- What do they do to continually grow and learn?

- Visualize what it would be like to serve in that role.

- What attracts you to this role? What would it feel like for you?

- How does this role reflect your core values?

After you have found some role models, use their answers to inspire you to write your own goals. Write your goals in present tense, as though you have already achieved them. This will help you visualize them with more clarity and confidence. You should create five to seven goals to help you achieve this segment of your Success Plan, and they should address most or all of the areas listed below. As you write your goals, be sure to visualize how it will look and feel to achieve them.

Areas of Your Career to Address with Your 10-Year Goals:

- Type of role and industry

- Level of leadership to achieve at the 10-year mark

- Work environment and atmosphere

- Work-life balance

- Income level

- Career growth opportunities that lie ahead

Example: Jane's 10-Year Goals

For example, let's say Jane wants to grow her income level and savings so she is able to buy a house within the next 10 years. In order to do this, she will need to increase her level of responsibility significantly. She knows that she wants to be in a leadership role in a large organization that offers additional career advancement opportunities. She also wants to help her coworkers advance their careers. Work-life balance is important to her, and she wants to have an active social life. In this scenario, Jane's 10-year goals would look something like this:

1. I am serving in a senior director role in a Fortune 500 organization in the financial industry, supervising a team of more than 15 professionals. I have an office with a beautiful view of the surrounding area.

2. My team respects me and is fully engaged in our work. I look for opportunities to help team members create their Success Plans and actively support them in achieving their goals.

3. I am preparing myself to advance to a vice president role within the next three years with my current employer. I have a mentor within the organization who advises me.

4. My income level has more than doubled and I have the opportunity to continue to advance my income through salary adjustments and bonuses.

5. I live in my dream city and have purchased a beautiful condo in a high-rise building located near a park where I run five mornings per week. I have a great circle of friends who enjoy the kinds of activities I do, and we frequently travel together.

It's easy to visualize the life Jane will be leading in 10 years through this list of goals, isn't it? The Success Plan Course provides guidance to help with creating your 10-year goals. Take some time with this. You are setting goals that will guide your 3- and 5-year goals, as well.

So, there you have it. After completing this work, you will have visualized and created concrete goals for where you will be with your career 10 years from today. Feels pretty empowering, doesn't it? And you can absolutely reach these goals if you stay focused and open to being successful.

It might be a good idea at this point to take a break and go celebrate what you just accomplished. Not only have you identified your core values and focus statement, but now you have a clear vision for where you will be in 10 years and specific goals to get you there. You are well on your way to completing your Success Plan!

Step 2: Your 5-Year Goals

If you've taken a break, and I strongly advise that you do, take a moment to review your 10-year goals and visualize your future. Now let's back up five years and create what it looks like to be halfway to that place. This process is a lot easier because you already know where you're heading with your career. Also, it makes the 10-year goals even more manageable because these goals support getting you halfway through your Success Plan. You're not starting from scratch!

As you read the next paragraph, be sure to visualize how all of this looks and feels. Really soak it up and imagine yourself at the 5-year mark of your Success Plan.

> *You are five years into achieving your 10-year career aspirations by now. Since you have learned a lot from your mentor and have an excellent start on creating your network, you know you are on the right course and have made smart moves with your current job and career. Your leader considers you one of her top performers and actively looks for ways to help you reach your goals. You have probably made one career move by now, possibly within the same organization. You have five more years until you reach your 10-year goals and fulfill your Success Plan. What do you need to have accomplished to be halfway there?*

Take some time to identify four to six goals you will need to achieve at the 5-year mark in order to be halfway to fulfilling your Success Plan. Once again, write them in present tense, as though you have already achieved them, and address most or all of the areas listed below.

Areas of Your Career to Address with Your 5-Year Goals:

- Level of role and responsibilities
- Network development
- Income level
- Performance metrics

- Value you bring to the organization
- Career ladder to reach your 10-year goals

Let's revisit Jane's scenario. We already know where she wants to be in 10 years. What would her goals look like at the halfway point? Probably something along the lines of the following example.

Example: Jane's 5-Year Goals

1. I am serving in a senior coordinator role in a Fortune 500 organization in the financial industry. This position offers me significant opportunities for growth within the organization.

2. My coworkers are fun to work with and we support each other in our duties. I have identified a mentor who is happy to help guide my career advancement.

3. I bring value to the organization by ensuring everything I do supports our strategic plan for growth and regularly report my achievements to my director.

4. My network has grown substantially. I have identified tiers of importance within my network and have a plan for remaining in regular contact and providing benefit accordingly.

5. My income level has increased by 40 percent and I am saving money in order to buy a condo in the city where I recently relocated.

Notice how these goals support Jane achieving her 10-year goals. It's easy to visualize how she will progress forward and what she needs to accomplish at the halfway mark to completing her Success Plan. I hope you are finding that setting goals is becoming easier and your future vision is getting clearer as you work through this process. Again, the Success Plan Course offers guidance to help with this process.

Step 3: Your 3-Year Goals

You are almost finished creating your Success Plan goals! Setting your 3-year goals will probably be easy since you now know where you want to be 10 years from today, and what you need to accomplish in 5 years in order to position yourself for success. Here's a 3-year-point visualization paragraph to help you get a sense of what's happening at that point:

Three years from today, you have a solid foothold on your career path and have made good progress in setting yourself up for future success. This is your "soak it up" phase, where you are focused on learning as much as you can from your leaders, coworkers, and the people you are adding to your network.

You may have transitioned from one position to another, or you're in the same role and taking on more responsibility as you prove your value to the organization. It's important to be patient at this point and remain focused on learning and observing as much as you can about your chosen field of work, as well as the leader attributes you admire and want to incorporate into your own leadership style. Remember that success often comes in small steps and very rarely, if ever, happens overnight!

OK, you know what to do next—create three to five goals to achieve within the next three years. Think of them as mile-markers you'll reach as you're heading to the halfway point to your 10-year goals. These are probably much less intimidating goals and should feel very achievable. As you know, they should be written in present tense, as though you have already achieved them. Be sure to include most or all of the areas listed below.

Areas of Your Career to Address with Your 3-Year Goals:

- Position status

- Lessons learned

- Network development

- Value you bring to the organization

- Positioning for advancement

What would Jane's goals look like for this point in her Success Plan? We know where she wants to be in five and ten years. In order to reach her 3-year mark, positioned to achieve her 5-year goals, she might create goals similar to this:

Example: Jane's 3-Year Goals

1. I have taken on additional duties in my coordinator role at a mid-sized organization in the financial industry. I am focused on learning as much as I can and advancing to the next level within the next two years at a larger employer in my dream city.

2. I have begun growing my network and have 50 local and virtual connections that I keep in contact with on a regular basis. I have monthly meet-ups with some of my local connections to build relationships.

3. I bring value to the organization by taking on special projects and helping my coworkers when needed. This enables me to learn even more and position myself strongly for my next career move.

4. I research the industry to identify my next employer and have made five connections in Fortune 500 organizations. I will join one of these organizations within the next two years.

It's important to create goals that address where you will be in three years, as well as how you are positioning yourself to reach your 5-year goals. Note how Jane has set goals that are linked to forward momentum. Everything is focused on learning and connecting to set herself up for success.

Step 4: Your Milestones to Success

In order to keep track of your progress toward achieving your goals, you will need to include measurable milestones for each of them. This will help motivate you to remain focused and feel a sense of achievement along the way. You will want to focus on the stage you are currently in when establishing milestones. Start with your 3-year goals and then address your 5-year goals once you are close to reaching your 3-year mark.

Let's use Jane's three-year goals as an example of how this works.

Jane's 3-Year Goals with Milestones:

- I have taken on additional duties in my coordinator role at a mid-sized organization in the financial industry. I am focused on learning as much as I can and advancing to the next level within the next two years at a larger employer in my dream city.

    o Milestones:

    - Obtained a coordinator role with one of my targeted employers.

    - Assigned three additional duties.

    - Promoted to a senior coordinator position.

- I have begun growing my network and have 50 local and virtual connections that I keep in contact with on a regular basis. I have monthly meet-ups with some of my local connections to build relationships.

    o Milestones:

    - I have 25 contacts in my network.

    - I have 50 contacts in my network.

    - Held four consecutive quarters of touchpoints with my virtual connections.

    - Attended 12 consecutive months of meet-ups with my local connections.

- I bring value to the organization by taking on special projects and helping my coworkers when needed. This enables me to learn even more and position myself strongly for my next career move.

    o Milestones:

        - Involved in four special projects either as a leader or team member.

        - Helped my coworkers with their assigned duties or projects five times over the course of three months.

- I research the industry to identify my next employer and have made five connections in Fortune 500 organizations. I will join one of these organizations within the next two years.

    o Milestones:

        - Completed research to identify five potential employers.

        - Made contact with an influencer at each of my five prospects.

        - Obtained a position with one of my five prospects.

You can see how breaking these goals down into measurable milestones makes them seem much more achievable, helping you focus on what you need to do next toward achieving your Success Plan. The milestones also help bring Jane's goals to life and make it easier to visualize success by adding tangible actions she can take along the way.

At this point, you are almost finished with your Success Plan. Next up is developing your personal marketing plan and determining how you will promote your most important product—yourself—to those you need to influence in order to accomplish your goals. This will probably have you thinking about things that haven't occurred to you in the past. The packaging and marketing of ourselves is something very few people ever take the time to think about. Another advantage to help set you apart from your peers!

CHAPTER 3: YOUR MARKETING PLAN

Even if marketing is not your chosen profession, you are a marketer promoting yourself. As your own "Chief Marketing Officer" (CMO), no one else but you is responsible for promoting and selling yourself to prospective employers, your leader, or your coworkers. This is a big responsibility that should be taken seriously. So, as your own CMO, you first need to create your marketing plan.

Part 1: Your Professional Brand Statement and Promise

The first step toward developing your marketing plan is to create your professional brand statement and promise. A professional brand statement is what you stand for, what people can expect from you, and what you intend to bring to your work, consistently, each and every day. A brand promise describes the way you will be perceived by coworkers and leaders when you consistently live according to your brand statement.

Fortunately, some of this work has already been done. So far in creating your Success Plan, you have identified your core values and focus statement, followed by a series of 3- 5- and 10-year goals. Develop your brand statement and promise based upon this work, specifically focused on your 10-year goals.

Let's review Jane's core values, focus statement, and 10-year goals from earlier in this section:

Jane's core values:

Finances, Growth, Achievement, Recognition, Excitement

Jane's focus statement:

My career path provides ample opportunities for increasing my salary and growing professionally. I am able to achieve great results and receive the recognition I deserve, which is exciting for me.

Jane's 10-year goals:

1. I am serving in a director-level role in a Fortune 500 organization in the financial industry, supervising a team of more than 15 professionals. I have an office with a beautiful view of the surrounding area.

2. My team respects me and is fully engaged in our work. I look for opportunities to help team members create their Success Plans and actively support them in achieving their goals.

3. I am preparing myself to advance to a vice president role within the next three years with my current employer. I have a mentor within the organization who advises me.

4. My income level has more than doubled and I have the opportunity to continue to advance my income through salary adjustments and bonuses.

5. I live in my dream city and have purchased a beautiful condo in a high-rise building located near a park where I run five mornings per week. I have a great circle of friends who enjoy the kinds of activities I do, and we frequently travel together.

You want to use your 10-year goals to develop your professional brand statement and promise because they reflect who and where you will ultimately be when you complete your Success Plan. Given that a professional brand statement is what you stand for, what people can expect from you, and what you intend to bring to your work, consistently, each and every day, Jane's statement might look something like this:

Jane's Professional Brand Statement:

> I am a dedicated professional focused on providing value to my employer, guidance for my team members, and the continual advancement of my career and income. I value working hard toward my goals and enjoying life in and outside of the workplace.

If Jane consistently lives up to her brand statement, her brand promise—how she is perceived by others in the workplace—might be as follows:

Jane's Brand Promise:

> I am a dedicated professional who stands out as a leader and brings value to my organization. I love what I do and enjoy life to my best ability.

You can see that this helps bring Jane's focus statement to life. Take some time in developing your professional brand statement and promise. Here's where you pull together everything you've done so far to create your Success Plan into one concise statement that describes your brand. This can be very powerful, so don't rush through it.

Once you have your brand statement and promise completed, you can begin working on the rest of your marketing plan. Following is an outline of the additional components you will need to include.

Part 2: Your Positioning Objectives

State what you want to achieve as a result of marketing yourself. How do you want to position yourself in the workplace? What can you do to promote your qualifications, dedication, and commitment to excellence? How will you stand out from your peers? What do you want others, especially leaders, to think of you? Positioning objectives are different from, yet related to, your goals. They reflect how you want to be perceived as you work toward achieving your goals.

Thinking this through and writing specific objectives to position yourself for success will help guide how you show up each day in the workplace. As with your 3-, 5-, and 10-year goals, they should be written in present tense, as though you have already achieved them. Let's look at what Jane's positioning objectives might include.

Jane's positioning objectives

- I am considered a leader among my peers and a rising star in the organization.

- I am accountable for my success and report key metrics on a regular basis.

- I can be relied upon to always meet deadlines and often go the extra mile to achieve goals.

- I lead my team with confidence and am focused on supporting their professional growth.

- I wear clothes that are professional, with a little flair to set myself apart from others.

Note that Jane has covered a nice range of areas in which to position herself, including the clothes that she wears. As you visualize yourself reaching your 10-year goals, how do you need to be positioned for success? Thinking through how you will do this is a key element of your success. And, again, this is something very few people consciously do.

Part 3: Your Target Audiences

This part addresses your target audiences—the people you are marketing yourself to. Although this might seem obvious, it's important to write down this list of key targets and be very clear about whom you want to impact with your positioning objectives. This will help you remain focused on the groups you need to interact with, and how, each day. Given Jane's positioning objectives, her target audiences would likely include the following:

Jane's list of target audiences

- Leaders in the organization: key leaders above my current level

- Peers in the organization: colleagues at the same level as me

- Team members: both my team and their peers

- Family members: parents and siblings

Note that Jane included her family as a target audience. If making your family proud of your professional accomplishments is important, add them to your list! Additional potential target audiences include board members, community leaders, your mentor, and any other person or groups that you want to positively influence. Be as specific as you can, even writing down names of key individuals to target with your marketing efforts.

Once you have your target audiences identified, take time on a monthly basis to reflect on what you have done to impact each audience and what you will do in the coming month in that regard. This will ensure that you remain focused on positioning yourself effectively on an ongoing basis. Also, know that this list will very likely change as you progress through your career. Keep your target list updated as needed.

Part 4: Your Tactics

You've developed your professional brand statement and promise, created a list of positioning objectives, and identified your target audiences. Excellent work! Now, to accomplish this, you'll need to develop a list of tactics. Tactics are the specific things you will do and actions you will take to achieve your positioning objectives and set yourself apart from your peers.

There are six areas I recommend you include in your tactics. You may identify additional areas to address, but make sure to include these at a minimum.

1. **Your Personal Presentation**—This is how you come across to others and what people see when they look at you, whether you interact with them or not. It includes your clothing, your body language, your makeup, your hair—everything that goes into making a first impression. By consciously thinking about how you want to be seen, you will proactively approach this important aspect of your professional brand. Your personal presentation tactics should address all of the elements that go into making a positive first impression.

2. **Your Level of Preparation**—Another important aspect of successful positioning is being prepared for work each day. One of the worst things you can do is to show up to a meeting without knowing what the objective of the meeting is, what you want to gain from it, and what you can contribute. Your preparation tactics might include always being sure to prepare as much

as possible ahead of each meeting or event in order to effectively add to the discussion, and taking the time to make a list of the questions you might have and what you want to get out of each meeting you have on a given day, etc. These actions will make you much more effective and position you very positively with your leaders, peers, and team members.

3. **Your Degree of Accountability**—You must be seen as keeping yourself accountable for your work product. You will have successes and failures at work (and in life!). You must take responsibility for both. Your accountability tactics might include celebrating your successes and learning from your mistakes. Perhaps a tactic could be sharing the glory of success with everyone who made it possible and never taking total credit for work in which others were involved. Conversely, another tactic could be taking appropriate responsibility for mistakes and failures.

   As you move into management, you are ultimately responsible for the work of your team members. Mistakes that happen under your watch are your mistakes, whether you were directly involved or not. Taking this approach toward being accountable will set you apart as a leader.

4. **Your Added Value**—Always bring some level of value to your interactions at work. Early in your career, it's OK to occasionally attend a meeting and say nothing. You're still in the learning stage and soaking up knowledge, so that's allowed. But don't let that happen very often. In order to avoid this, your added value tactics could include taking a lot of notes in meetings so you can add value in some way. For example, if there is a list of follow-up actions from the meeting, offer to take one on. Talk with your leader afterwards and offer to send her your notes.

As you progress in your career, set tactics to make sure you are focused on creating value each day. Always look for ways to be of value to your leader, peers, and team members. One tactic to accomplish this might be to review your calendar each morning and list out what you will do throughout the day to provide value to the meetings, projects, and assignments you will be involved in. Making this a disciplined habit each day will definitely set you apart from your peers.

5. **Your Elevator Speech**—This is a concise summary of what you want others to know about you. It's called an elevator speech because it should be something you could say in a short period of time, like the time required to take an elevator from the first floor to the fifth floor. Think of it as an introductory statement you will use when meeting someone for the first time. First impressions are vitally important to managing your personal brand. By preparing your elevator speech ahead of time, you will nail that first impression. If you don't, you could easily miss out on making a positive impact on an important contact, make no impact at all and quickly be forgotten, or worse, you could make a negative impact and be remembered for it. Yikes!

   Your elevator speech should not be too self-serving or boastful. It should include things like your role, a bit about your background, and perhaps something important you are working on. You will want to update it as you progress through your career, of course. Keep in mind that, along with your personal presentation, your elevator speech can help you make a great first impression. Following is an example, based on Jane's positioning objectives.

Jane's Positioning Objectives

- I am considered a leader among my peers and a rising star in the organization.

- I am accountable for my success and report key metrics on a regular basis.

- I can be relied upon to always meet deadlines and often go the extra mile to achieve goals.

- I lead my team with confidence and am focused on supporting their professional growth.

- I wear clothes that are professional, with a little flair to set myself apart from others.

Jane's elevator speech

I am currently serving in a role that enables me to make a positive impact on the organization, which is very important to me. For example, our most recent report on key metrics showed a positive trend for the year and 10 percent growth toward our strategic initiatives over the past six months. I've been here three years now and look forward to continuing to grow with the organization. *And don't you just love the shoes I'm wearing?*

Well, maybe leave that last sentence about the shoes out, but you get the drift! Think about how you can keep your elevator speech updated and relevant with references to current projects and results.

6. **Your Daily Interview**—Each day, in everything that you do, you are interviewing for your next opportunity. Always keep this in mind. Your daily interview tactics should include approaching each day and every interaction like you would if it were an interview for an important career move. You never know when a key leader is sizing you up and considering whether you are ready for either a promotion or for an assignment on an important project that could help progress your career.

   All of the tactics listed above come together into this one. Visualize yourself nailing your personal presentation, being prepared for each part of your day, being appropriately accountable for your successes and mistakes, adding value to each interaction you have, and using your elevator speech when you meet new people. If you do all of this on a consistent basis, you will position yourself for exceptional success.

Sure, you will have an occasional "off" day where you just aren't performing at your best. Set tactics to address this to keep yourself focused on your work and avoid coming across in a negative light. Work toward making off days the exception.

Once you have developed the tactics you will implement to achieve your positioning objectives, you can get started on the final component of your marketing plan: how you will measure your success.

Part 5: Measurement and Tracking

There's an old marketing saying that states, "If you can't measure it, it's not worth doing." Just like you set milestones to track your progress toward your 3-year goals, it's important to determine how you will measure your progress toward achieving your positioning objectives. This is not as easy as tracking sales of a product or the return on a marketing investment; it will take some thought to create your measures of success. Work toward having two or three for each of your objectives.

Let's reflect on Jane's positioning objectives and consider what measures she might put in place to track her success toward achieving them.

> Jane's positioning objectives with measures of success

- I am considered a leader among my peers and a rising star in the organization.
    - Measures:
        - Annual performance evaluation
        - Quarterly informal feedback from my leader regarding my performance
        - Number of important projects assigned to me

- I am accountable for my success and report key metrics on a regular basis.

  o Measures:

    - Monthly reports on key metrics

    - Improvements made based upon results

- I can be relied upon to always meet deadlines and often go the extra mile to achieve goals.

  o Measures:

    - Percent of the time I meet my deadlines

    - Percent of the time I completed work prior to the assigned deadline

    - Examples of doing more than was expected on projects and assignments

- I lead my team with confidence and am focused on supporting their professional growth.

  o Measures:

    - Feedback from team members on my management style

    - Percent of team members with goals for the year, quarter, and month

    - Feedback from leaders on how my team is performing

- I wear clothes that are professional, with a little flair to set myself apart from others.

- Measures:
  - Compliments from others
  - Level of confidence I feel about my appearance

As with your milestones for your 3-year goals, these measures help you focus on what you need to do to achieve your positioning objectives. The more clearly you can visualize what you are working toward, the more likely you can complete your Success Plan with ease. The Success Plan Course provides guidance that can help make this process easier to complete!

The next chapter provides guidance on how and why to visualize success, as well as why it is essential that you focus on reaching your goals while giving up "the how." This is a very important part of the Success Plan process, so be sure to spend time soaking up everything in chapter four!

CHAPTER 4: VISUALIZING SUCCESS AND GIVING UP "THE HOW"

As discussed earlier in this section, just before you began identifying your 10-year goals, your success depends largely on believing in yourself, clearly visualizing where you want to be at each stage of your Plan, and giving up "the how"—trusting that the specifics of how you will achieve your lofty and aggressive goals will come to you when the time is right. Sounds a little weird and intangible, but it works!

Your Visualization Process

In order to remain focused on your goals, you must consistently visualize achieving them. Each day, take time out to review the goals you are currently working toward, whether it's your 3-, 5-, or 10-year set of goals. Keep them handy and easy to locate so you won't put off this vitally important process.

Follow these steps for effective daily visualization:

Goal Visualization Technique

- Find about 15 minutes in your day, preferably in the morning before the day gets away from you and you're off to the races.

- Get into a comfortable spot where you won't be interrupted.

- Pull up the list of goals you are currently working toward and read each one, out loud if possible.

- Close your eyes and visualize achieving each goal individually. Put yourself in the place you will be once you achieve the goal—what are your surroundings like? Who is with you?

- Think about how it will feel to achieve the goal and the emotions you will experience. Are you happy? Proud? Exhilarated?

- Spend about three or five minutes visualizing each goal, then move to the next one.

It's a fairly simple process but it might feel awkward at first. Stick with it. The more frequently and consistently you practice your visualization technique, the more quickly you will move forward to achieve your goals.

While you will visualize your immediate goals daily, you don't want to lose sight of your longer-term goals. You will need to set aside time to go through this process with your next set of goals, as well, but on a less frequent basis. You get to determine the cadence for visualizing your longer-term goals. Monthly might feel right, or you might find that quarterly works better. Whatever you decide, simply go through the visualization technique for your immediate goal, say your 3-year goals, and then immediately follow the same process for your 5-year goals. It will take longer on the day you choose to do both, obviously, so make sure you have time set aside to complete the entire process.

Periodically review your entire set of goals, as well, so you are keeping your longest-term goals top of mind. For example, if you are visualizing your 3- and 5-year goals every other month, take time to visualize the entire set including your 10-year goals every quarter. Put reminders on your calendar in order to be disciplined about this. Consistent visualization is very important to your ultimate success.

Giving up "The How"

As you visualize the achievement of your goals, don't be tempted to think about *how* you will achieve them. If you keep your mind focused on success and how it looks and feels, "the how" will naturally come to you.

You have probably experienced this in your life. It feels like an "aha moment" with inspiration or answers seemingly coming out of nowhere. Take a moment and think about a time when this happened for you. It was pretty powerful, wasn't it? You may have instantly come up with a way to solve a problem you had been working on for a while. Maybe it was the answer to something you had given up on solving.

If you allow yourself to focus on the how too early, you will get off track and delay reaching your goals. All you have to do is focus on success, not how you will succeed. Trust that the how will show up.

Insights: Kathleen's Take on Section 1

Kathleen is a phenomenal woman that I have had the honor of working with for several years. In her twenties, she created a digital marketing firm that has now grown into a significant player in the industry. Her dedication to client relationships and the importance of focusing on results wins the confidence of the organizations she serves. She has been an inspiration to me in so many ways.

> *I asked Kathleen to review the first section of this book and provide feedback. Following are excerpts from her response:*
>
> *"I think it is important to identify values as well as to figure out what your strengths are and what motivates you. Being able to convey this to your leader is essential in developing good relationships at work. I like that you break goal setting down and start with 10 years. When you are thinking that far in advance, it is easier to not let the 'how' get in your way.*
>
> *"Being the CMO of your own brand is very important. I think women really struggle with this because we never want to seem to brag or be boastful. Perhaps not all women feel this way, but I definitely struggle with it.*
>
> *"I really like the tactics included in the marketing plan. I completely agree with each of them, especially being prepared. I always tell my team that I have never regretted being over prepared.*
>
> *"I also appreciate how you mention the importance of continuing to visualize your long-term goals. I think it so easy to get caught up in the daily details and lose your focus on the future. Regularly looking up and forward is important."*

Celebrate!

At this point, you have created your Success Plan to guide your career for the next 10 years! This is something very few people do, and it will give you such an advantage as you work toward achieving your goals and advancing your career. This is something to celebrate in whatever way you find enjoyable—dinner with friends, relaxing in the park, happy hour, fill in the blank! Be sure to congratulate yourself and soak up what you've accomplished. This is a BIG deal!

The next section will provide guidance on a range of topics to help navigate your Success Plan as effectively as possible. I will cover how to attract success, learn and network for success, and balance your career with your personal life. Additionally, there's a discussion on shifting your focus roughly every ten years throughout your career. You start out in the learning phase and ultimately shift into mentoring. It's important to identify which phase you are in so you can shift your focus accordingly. After you've celebrated the creation of your Success Plan, meet me in section two and let's get started!

SECTION 2:
GUIDANCE FOR SUCCESS

• •

If you're starting this section, you have completed your Success Plan. Congratulations on taking a positive, proactive, and very important step toward creating your future! As I've stated, this is something very few people ever take the time to do. Creating and following your Success Plan—making adjustments along the way and staying focused on your goals—will position you to achieve whatever you visualize. You are heading into an exciting phase of your career! The next three years will form the foundation for reaching your 5- and 10-year goals.

This section provides guidance as you implement your Success Plan. Each sub-section gives specific Success Tips and either new or affirmed knowledge that will support your success and help differentiate you among your peers. All of this is based upon what I have learned throughout my career, from my personal experiences as well as observing others and being committed to continual learning.

SUCCESS TIP 1: ATTRACTING SUCCESS— THE LAW OF ATTRACTION

• •

Can you really *attract* success into your life? You absolutely can. You simply have to be very clear about what success looks like for you and remain focused on it. And since you just created your Success Plan with your 3-, 5-, and 10-year goals along with clear visualizations for each of them, you are ready to activate the Law of Attraction . . . actually, you already have.

The Law of Attraction, in its simplest form, states that "like attracts like" and what you think about and focus on becomes your reality. It is important to note that the Law of Attraction is working right now in your life and has been since you started thinking on your own. It's like the Law of Gravity; it works whether we understand it or not, and it's always there. So, if the Law of Attraction is in motion even when we don't realize it—bringing opportunities, people, and situations to us based upon what we think about and focus on—just imagine what you could accomplish if you harnessed that power and utilized it to your best advantage!

Personal Story: The Law of Attraction in Action

The Law of Attraction worked during the process I went through to realize that I wanted to create this book. This was never something I thought about doing. Writing a book was nowhere on my radar, ever.

I reached a stage in my life and career where I felt like I had extra capacity. Deep inside, I knew I should be doing something more—not something else, but something additional. So, having recently learned about the Law of Attraction, I decided to put it to work and I set an intentional goal to figure out what that "something additional" was. I thought about it on a daily basis and kept my mind positive and open to hints and guidance from opportunities, people, and situations.

Over a period of two or three months, I gradually become very clear on what I would do, and why. I realized that one of the things I enjoy most is helping early- and mid-career professionals grow and realize their full potential. I thought about how I had been doing this most of my career and always enjoyed it. But I was not intentional about it or focused on it—it just happened. Over thirty years, I probably helped a dozen people in this way. And it occurred to me how small that number was!

Suddenly it was crystal clear what that "something additional" would be. I would intentionally help people, specifically women, grow professionally. I would help them create a plan to guide their career path. It would be called a Success Plan, and I would do this on a large scale, rather than one-on-one. By doing this, I would be able to give back based upon my years of experience and make a positive impact on thousands of women. Wow! This was both amazing and frightening! I had no idea how to make this vision a reality.

So, I called upon the Law of Attraction once more. I thought about my new vision every day and waited for more inspiration. I talked with people I respected and whose input I valued. They loved the idea and encouraged me to make it happen. Their support helped me remain focused and open to what would come next. Writing this book suddenly popped into my mind one day, and though I thought it made sense, I had no idea how to write a book and get it published. It seemed like a crazy idea, but I knew it was somehow possible. After doing some research I was relieved to find an online resource that could guide me along the way, and that's when I started on the journey of creating this book. It all happened according to the Law of Attraction. What you focus on and visualize with conviction really will become your reality!

I am sure you can think of instances in your life where something like this happened for you. Maybe on a smaller scale, or something even more significant. Perhaps deciding what you wanted to major in while attending college. It could have been achieving your personal best in athletics, something you visualized and focused on for a period of time. Whatever your example, it was the Law of Attraction working on your behalf, probably without you even realizing it.

By reading my personal story of how the Law of Attraction helped guide me and thinking about how it has worked in your own life, you should now understand how you can attract into your life opportunities, people, and situations that are in keeping with your thoughts. You can, therefore, create whatever you want in your career by setting clear goals and visualizing how success looks and feels and remaining focused on it—which is what your Success Plan is all about!

Note that I emphasize remaining focused on success. This is extremely important. Don't make the mistake of creating your Success Plan, celebrating your accomplishment, and then filing it away and only looking at it once in a while. That would be tragic and a complete waste of the time and energy you just put into creating your Success Plan. You have to keep your Success Plan top of mind, all the time. You must visualize the goals you are working toward on a regular basis (daily, like I did) so that the Law of Attraction can work in your favor.

There is a lot of literature supporting and explaining the Law of Attraction in detail. I strongly recommend researching this topic as much as you need to in order to fully comprehend the amazing impact it can have on your success. As you learned from reading my personal story, I have seen it in action and utilizing it to my advantage has enabled me to help you with your Success Plan and have the opportunity to help thousands of women succeed in their careers. Pretty powerful stuff!

Attracting Success Through Gratitude

Another way to attract success into your life through the Law of Attraction is to develop a gratitude practice. This helps you remain positive and appreciative of everything you have, right now. Remember, like attracts like. If you are generally positive in your approach to your work, you will attract positive projects and supportive people. If you are negative, you are sabotaging yourself—you become your own worst enemy and you will not be successful to your full potential. It simply is not possible. I have observed this in others and experienced it myself, firsthand.

To create a gratitude practice, keep a gratitude journal and write down what you appreciate in your life on a regular basis. Stop throughout the day to realize and acknowledge what you appreciate and take a moment to jot it down. This can be something as simple as the way your dog is happy to see you when you get home, or beautiful weather, or finding that perfect shade of lipstick. It could also be something big, like landing that new job, nailing an important presentation, or realizing that you just achieved all of your 3-year goals! The big things are easy to identify; the smaller ones take more thought and intention but can actually have a greater impact on your level of positivity because they are surrounding you all the time—you just need to let yourself notice them.

By simply taking the time on a regular basis to think about all the things you have to be grateful for, you will become more and more positive, and this will spill over into your work life. Positive people, opportunities, and situations will be attracted to you. You will learn how important it is to surround yourself with positivity.

What's interesting is that after you do this for a while, negativity will probably begin to feel toxic. You will likely have no tolerance for being around negative people and situations. I compare it to cigarette smoke. As a non-smoker, I can't tolerate being around it. I don't like the way it smells and I know it's not healthy to breathe in. Negativity has the same effect on me. I don't like the way it feels and I know it will distract me from my goals. I avoid it whenever possible, and I have been excited to see this sort of shift away from negativity happen for other people, most significantly my daughter, Blaire! After a life-changing mission trip, she learned the importance of being surrounded by positivity.

Real-Life Vignette: Blaire's Journey to Positivity

Blaire was always fairly positive and happy throughout her childhood. She had negative moments during her teenage years, just like everyone else. But it wasn't until after graduating college and taking a mission trip to Thailand and Laos that she realized how wonderful it feels to be surrounded by positivity. She spent a month with a group of her peers on the trip, all of whom were strangers to her on day one, but like-minded in that they wanted to make a positive contribution to others. Over the course of the next 30 days, they were immersed in the Thai and Lao cultures. They witnessed people with almost no material possessions being happier and more positive than many of the people they knew back home.

The group she was traveling with was made up of positive people who supported each other during their daily tasks, working together to help the local villagers. Spending a month with that group, getting to know them, and soaking up all the positivity was life-changing for Blaire. She was able to experience the personal impact of remaining positive and being surrounded by positive people. She made lifelong friends and learned a lot about herself and how to connect in a meaningful way with others.

When she returned from the trip, she quickly realized that she could not tolerate negativity at all! She avoids negative people and situations and keeps her thoughts positive as much as possible. And because of this, the Law of Attraction has been working overtime for her. It has been wonderful to watch her attract positive people and opportunities into her life since that mission trip. She began a career in her chosen profession and made tremendous strides toward building a solid foundation during her first year. Of course, a lot of her success is due to her talents and abilities, but I believe her positive approach to life has played a significant role in it, as well.

Here are some tips for remaining positive and avoiding negativity in the workplace:

- If you find yourself in negative conversations at work—like gossiping or complaining—change the discussion to something productive and positive. Look for the positive aspect of the situation. If others don't take your lead, politely remove yourself from the discussion.

- Avoid toxic people. They will do nothing but harm and can have a negative impact on the goals you have established in your Success Plan. They're easy to identify. They are rarely, if ever, happy and usually find something to complain about in every situation. Figure out who they are in your workplace and avoid them as much as possible.

- If you have to work closely with a negative person, prepare yourself ahead of time so you can deflect their comments and complaints. Keep your thoughts positive and remain focused on what you are working toward in your Success Plan. Who knows, by setting a positive example, you might help them lose some of their negative habits!

- If you tend to lean toward the negative, you have some work to do. The good news is that you can retrain yourself to move away from your own negativity! Each day, work toward shifting to a positive way of thinking by starting a gratitude practice and stopping yourself from complaining whenever the urge hits. You'll be so glad you did. And your Success Plan will thank you!

I can't over-emphasize the importance of harnessing the Law of Attraction by remaining focused on your goals and keeping your thoughts and actions positive. This is absolutely vital to your success. Make it your top priority.

Attracting Success by Creating the Culture You Want (Even If It's a Micro-Culture)

This might sound hard to believe, but you can make an incredible impact on the culture of your workplace, no matter the level of your position. Each person in a given organization plays an important part in creating the atmosphere in the workplace. You can help create the culture you want by your actions and how you show up each day. In fact, your work environment can feel very different to you than it might to your coworkers. You can create your own "micro-culture," as you follow your Success Plan and stay positive, that deflects any negativity in the workplace by simply ignoring it and refusing to let others' behavior impact your outlook.

Real-Life Vignette: Angie's Micro-Culture

I had the honor of working with Angie for about four years. Her approach to what was a very difficult working environment with ever-changing direction, continual crises, limited resources, and very demanding internal clients was nothing less than inspirational. She had every reason to give in to the negativity that became somewhat rampant within the organization due to constant turmoil, ongoing reductions in force, and a lot of leadership turnover. But she chose not to, and I'm certain that was a choice she had to consciously make each day.

Angie created her own micro-culture, and it was the first time I had witnessed this in action. She kept her thoughts positive and stayed out of the rumor mill as much as possible. When she found herself involved in a negative conversation, she pointed out the positive aspects of the situation under discussion and helped shift things to the positive. When she felt stretched due to the lack of resources and ever-increasing workload, instead of complaining she said, "The work is the work; we will get it done."

Because of her approach, people were drawn to her and thought very highly of her—not only as a colleague or coworker, but as a person. Team members within the department often sought her guidance in dealing with difficult people and situations. Even though she was very busy, she always took the time to talk with them and help find a solution to whatever was troubling them. She was seen as a shining star in the department and organization. And she was highly respected by leadership.

Angie's micro-culture was pretty amazing to experience. I learned a lot from her and since the time she and I worked together, I have made a point of carrying her approach forward. It has proven to be one of the key learnings of my career.

Think about it. You have a Success Plan which will guide you to achieving your 10-year goals. You know that your current role is a means to the end of achieving what you want in your career. Most people don't have a Success Plan, so it's easy to start complaining when work becomes difficult or workplace policies don't seem fair, or so-and-so gets paid more but doesn't work as hard, etc. Yuck. It's a downward spiral that is difficult to climb out of, to be certain.

Others can be in that downward spiral, but you don't have to join them, right? Absolutely not. And by remaining positive and focused and avoiding the office complaint pool, you will be noticed by good leaders and very likely become involved in projects and opportunities that will help you reach your goals even faster than you planned. And you will have a lot more fun each day as well.

Your Professional Success and Happiness— Who is Responsible?

Another way of thinking that can be disruptive to your success as well as your positive micro-culture is believing that your employer and leader are responsible for your professional success and happiness. This is simply not true. Your employer is responsible for hiring you and providing a safe environment in which to work. Your leader is responsible for providing constructive feedback to help you hone your skills and grow professionally, and she needs to make sure you are productive at work. That's a lot, but that is about the extent of their responsibility.

Contrast: Jane vs. Audrey

We've learned a lot about Jane through the course of this book. We know that she is very career-minded but enjoys a good work/life balance. We know what her 3-, 5-, and 10-year goals are, and we know how she plans to measure her progress toward reaching her goals.

Let's get to know Audrey, a new character. She and Jane have similar goals. She has a lot going for her—an advanced degree from a prestigious university, a wide network of contacts that includes some heavy-hitters in some of the top organizations in her industry, and a very strong work ethic. Jane and Audrey have a lot in common . . . until it comes to one very important quality. Personal responsibility. Audrey doesn't take personal responsibility and didn't create a Success Plan.

While Jane focuses on her Success Plan, visualizing what it will be like to achieve her goals and acting on the inspirational "how" moments that come to her, Audrey generally sits around with a pissed off attitude. She doesn't understand why her employer isn't fulfilling her desires for advancement. She begins to think the leaders are not very bright. Audrey and a circle of co-complainers share jokes about the decisions upper management makes, finding fault in almost every new initiative they introduce to help achieve the organization's strategic goals. She has given up responsibility for her success and happiness to an employer she does not respect. What a waste of talent and capability. She's in a professional death spiral.

Meanwhile, Jane is focused on success. Would you rather be Jane or Audrey?

You are responsible for your professional success and happiness. You are responsible for your individual successes and failures, and what you learn from each. You are the one who decides to approach work from a positive or negative perspective. You are the *only one* who can create and implement your Success Plan.

It is very important to realize where the responsibility for your success lies. If you give it to someone else, you will drift through your career rather than taking control of it and getting where you want to be professionally, in the timeframe you have identified. This can be a bit confronting to realize, but I invite you to be empowered by this knowledge. If you accept that you are responsible for implementing your Success Plan, no one can keep you from being successful. It's really as simple as that.

SUCCESS TIP 2:
LEARNING FOR SUCCESS—
INVEST IN YOURSELF

• •

One of the most important things you can do to achieve the goals in your Success Plan is to continually invest in yourself by learning new skills and obtaining new knowledge. I cannot overstate the importance of continual learning. By applying and mastering new skills, you make yourself more valuable. In fact, your next opportunity might hinge on whether you are positioned with the additional knowledge and skills required to be successful in the role.

Don't wait for your employer to offer opportunities for enhanced learning—seek them out and bring them to your leader for consideration. If she cannot pay for a given opportunity due to budget constraints or other obstacles, don't stop there. Consider investing in the opportunity yourself if it provides value to your future. Think of it this way: if you are not planning on remaining with your current employer for an extended period of time, should you really hold the organization responsible for paying for all of your continual learning opportunities? Probably not. And is it fair to you to let a no from your organization keep you from taking advantage of a key learning opportunity? No, it's definitely not. Remember you are responsible for your ultimate success. No one else.

You can find other ways to gain value from your employer if they don't have the funds to support a learning opportunity. For example, if you find yourself paying to attend a conference on your own, consider negotiating with your leader so you do not have to take vacation time in order to attend. Or if you are taking some courses at a local college that require you to miss time from work, negotiate to avoid taking paid time off while in class. After all, you will probably be using the knowledge you gain from these learning opportunities in your current role. Doing these things can turn the situation around to benefit both you and your employer.

One rule of thumb for investing in yourself for continual learning is to spend three to five percent of your annual income on learning opportunities. This can include conferences and courses, as discussed, and also books, audio books, online courses, and other learning opportunities. Proactively setting aside funds each month to use toward strengthening your knowledge and skills will help ensure your success in the long run. A little sacrifice goes a long way in this instance!

If you choose not to invest in yourself, not only do you become stagnant, but you actually decrease your value over time. As new advances and disruptive technologies are developed in your field of work, you need to embrace them and learn as much as you can. If you don't, you'll be left in the dust of your colleagues who are proactively growing and learning!

Decision Point: Advanced Degree?

The decision regarding whether to pursue an advanced degree depends largely on your Success Plan and your field of work. If you want to rise in the ranks of leadership to perhaps a vice president or chief officer role, you will most likely need an advanced degree. Many employers will not consider candidates without these credentials for roles above the manager level. Do some research in your industry and find out what might be required in order to reach your goals.

Advanced degrees can also help when negotiating a higher salary. Pay ranges might differ for those with advanced degrees. The teaching profession is one where this is typically the case, and there are others. Ask some questions of your human resources representative to learn more about this for your industry.

Some women choose to obtain a master's degree immediately after completing their undergraduate degree, prior to conducting their first job search. This is a good idea if your industry is very competitive and advanced degrees are expected, even at entry levels. Others take some time to determine whether an advanced degree is essential to success.

Personal Story: My Decision to Obtain an MBA

Early in my career, I never considered going back to school to earn an advanced degree. I just didn't think it was necessary and really didn't consider whether my future success might be hampered if I didn't have one. After 15 years of working in the healthcare marketing field, I had advanced about as far as I could with my undergraduate degree—a Bachelor of Fine Arts. I was working at the director level in a healthcare organization and realized advancement from there would be difficult without a master's degree.

I decided to complete an executive MBA program at a local university, which meant attending classes in the evenings and spending time away from my family to complete assignments and participate in group projects over a two-year period. Fortunately for me, my family was very supportive and we were able to manage the tuition and time away from family activities without a lot of sacrifice. If these two factors weren't in place, it could have been a much more stressful experience.

As I have mentioned a few times during the course of this book, I never created a Success Plan for myself. I sort of drifted into the realization that I wanted to advance to the next level and that I needed a master's degree. However, if I had taken the time to think through where I was headed, I might have moved forward in my career in less time than I ultimately did.

Take some time to conduct the appropriate research and think through whether an advanced degree makes sense for you, and if so, when. Maybe this is already a part of your Success Plan, or maybe it should be an addition. Don't simply drift into it like I did! Be proactive.

More Tips on Learning

These tips will help you stay focused on learning—outside of a formal education environment. Consider that each day brings a wealth of opportunities for you to learn and soak up important information and experiences that will lead to the fulfillment of your Success Plan. If you are in the learning stage of your career, these tips will be exceptionally important. However, they apply to all stages of your career. No one knows everything, ever!

1. **Early in your career, or in a new position, feel good about asking a lot of questions.** This is expected and appreciated. Your leader and coworkers should not expect you to know everything starting on day 1, or 51, or 101! Of course, try not to ask the same questions multiple times! Take notes and soak up the information you are gathering. Apply new knowledge as quickly as you can in order to retain it effectively. It is always better to ask questions than to assume you know how to do something. Ultimately, you will learn more quickly and complete projects more efficiently. And this will be noticed by your leader.

2. **Listen more than you speak—never speak more than you listen.** This is very important, especially early in your career, and might be a little difficult for the extroverts among us! Even at this stage in my career, I much prefer to listen and observe when in new situations. We learn so much more by listening than by speaking! Listen for content and learning, observe for context

and application. Most people enjoy talking and being asked to share their knowledge. They might even feel flattered that you chose to ask them for information and insights. Use this aspect of human nature to your advantage and soak up everything you can.

3. **Learn how to get into the room.** By this, I mean learn how to get invited to meetings that will benefit you from a learning perspective. Early in your career, when your leader makes a presentation that the team has been working on for weeks, ask if you can accompany her to take notes and write down questions that require follow-up. After you have more experience, ask to present a part of the presentation. Assert that this will be helpful in strengthening your presentation skills and enhance your value to the organization. At some point, you will be the one making the full presentation, so gaining experience will be important.

4. **Learn how to read the room.** Ah, now this one is very important. By reading the room, I mean learning how to understand what is going on under and over the words being spoken in a given meeting. Observe things like who is in charge of the meeting and how she is accepted by others in the room. Do they respect her? Does she manage the meeting well? What might you do the same or differently if you were in charge of the meeting? Are the ideas being shared generally accepted by the attendees, or not? This is all about understanding the environment in which you work, the acceptable norms of behavior, and so forth. Taking the time to conduct this informal research can benefit your upward mobility. You'll commit fewer missteps and enjoy more "nailed it" experiences!

To sum things up, continual learning is vital to your ongoing success and to the fulfillment of your Success Plan. This can be done formally through conferences and courses and informally through asking questions, listening, and observing what is going on around you. Commit to investing in yourself with 3 to 5 percent of your income. This will get you farther, faster. And so will effective networking, which is what we will dive into next!

SUCCESS TIP 3: NETWORKING FOR SUCCESS

••

Networking is an essential skill that I did not fully appreciate until later in my career. It takes time and intentional nurturing to build your network of contacts and mentors, as well as those you mentor. By starting a focused networking program early in your career, you will create a circle of valuable resources and reach your goals much faster and more effectively.

And now networking is easier than ever, given all the ways we can stay connected through digital and social media. Social platforms, like LinkedIn, Facebook, and Instagram, along with texting and email make it very easy to connect with members of your network on a regular basis. Telephone conversations and in-person meetings require more time but are invaluable and can be the most effective way to remain connected.

So, how do you get started? Chances are, you already have. You probably have a circle of friends, family, and friends-of-the-family who provide support and guidance to you already. You likely have added coworkers and leaders to your informal list. If you haven't done so at this point, it's time to formalize your network and pull all their contact information into one file. I use Excel because it's easy to navigate and sort, and I can add tabs for my categories of contacts. You might have another method—use what is best for your organization style.

Setting Up Your Network

First, go through your current informal list of contacts, which will likely come from multiple sources. Scour through your contacts on LinkedIn, Facebook, and Instagram and pull together those who could be helpful to you from a career perspective. Did you know that LinkedIn allows you to download your list of network connections into Excel? Using this as a starting point and then filling in additional contacts from other sources gives you a great head start. Add others from additional sources, like the contacts on your smart phone, your coworkers, and leaders, etc. The idea is to pull every applicable contact into one place, with name, email, phone number, employer, current position, links to social media profiles, and anything else you might want to include.

Once you have your initial list, you will want to begin categorizing them into groups, based upon the influence they can have on your career and support or guidance they may be able to provide. Rank them into high, medium, and low groups and separate them into tabs (if using Excel) or some other means of categorization. Add columns or fields to keep track of the date you last contacted them and the outcome.

Your "high" group, people who can definitely help advance your career, will probably be a fairly small number. You will want to contact them frequently—monthly or every two months. Make sure to have a good reason for reaching out—an update on how things are going with your job, a question they could help answer, or even an article you think they might find of interest. Try to make your outreach mutually valuable in some way.

Your "medium" group will be made up of people who are valuable to you as well, just not as important in helping you reach your goals as the "high" group. This group might include people you are helping or supporting with their goals, perhaps you are mentoring some of them. You will want to reach out to them each quarter, possibly more frequently based on your relationship with them and their proximity to you. But at least quarterly you should contact them with information that has meaning for your career, or theirs.

Your "low" group includes people you know and don't want to lose touch with but hold little value in helping you reach your career goals. They might be friends from college or people you know socially. There is no specific cadence for reaching out to this group. You will probably do this naturally since they tend to be social contacts. It's just helpful to keep them on your list for easy reference and you never know when one of them might become more valuable as a contact due to a career advancement or some other factor.

Once you have them sorted into groups, you are ready to begin a program of consistent outreach. Be disciplined about this—don't let it get away from you. Keep the groups small to begin with so this is manageable as you get used to reaching out and keeping track of the details.

Make it easier to maintain your network connections by using technology as your prompt to reach out, as well as a resource for content. One example is to sign up for a Google Alert related specifically to one of your contacts. This could be a given topic, area of interest, or particular organization of interest to her. You set the frequency of how often you want Google to email content related to your search criteria. Then automatically in your inbox you receive a list of relative links to news, websites, and events that are relevant to her. From here, you can simply copy/paste the information to your contact with a note saying why you felt she may find it interesting.

Regularly reaching out will be an important habit to form in order to keep yourself top of mind with people who can make a difference in your professional life.

> ### Real-Life Vignette: Jessica's Network
>
> *I met Jessica several years ago as a vendor partner. Throughout our relationship and even now, she provides me with interesting examples of programs from other organizations and industry-related news or events, and connects me with others in our industry that she believes I would appreciate knowing because of a shared interest or professional goal. Her outreach is never an attempt to sell me something or gain anything in return, but simply because she thought I would appreciate the information . . . and I did!*
>
> *In the time since Jessica and I worked together she has experienced changes in her career, both planned and unplanned. These changes evolved into many new and very exciting opportunities. One of the most significant came after an unplanned job change. When her organization was sold and her role was eliminated, she found herself on the job market without warning. Rather than feeling upset or down, she embraced it as an opportunity to reconnect and strengthen her network relationships.*
>
> *Over the next 30 days she made a list of her contacts and prioritized them based on their connection to the type of role or organizations she was targeting. From there, she took the time to send each a personalized note to see how they were doing and if they would have time to catch up via phone or in person in the near*

future. As her network started to respond, her calendar started to fill up with multiple phone calls and in-person meetings.

During the conversation, she listened intently for ways that she may be able to help her network member with additional professional connections, resources, or ideas. Despite her need for a new job, she did not make the conversation about that goal, but rather how she could connect and strengthen her relationship with each contact. This focus on the person and how she could support them encouraged her network to want to help her in return through additional introductions and opportunities.

In less than 60 days, she not only had multiple competing job offers, but also had nearly doubled her network connections! Since this time Jessica has continued to nurture her relationships through regular personal outreach. A few of her contacts have since found themselves looking for a job. Using this as an opportunity to pay it forward, she made the effort to match them to others that may be able to help.

By not focusing on her needs, but rather on the person and how she could help them, Jessica has some of the strongest network relationships I have seen. Her investment and focus on her network ties has paid off. She recently started her own business, and her network is there to support her by investing in her continued success.

Additional Networking Tips

1. **Find an Online Community**

Another way to network with peers and people with similar interests is to join an online community dedicated to a topic, cause, or movement that interests you. Conduct research to see what is available.

2. **Join Professional Organizations**

   There are probably professional organizations in your chosen career field that offer opportunities for education and networking. By maintaining memberships in such organizations and seeking leadership opportunities, you are building a resume that says you are dedicated to your profession and are leadership material.

3. **Use Every Meeting as a Networking Opportunity**

   Consider each meeting you attend within your organization to be an opportunity to build your network. Attend meetings with the goal in mind to initiate or strengthen an existing relationship with someone. The more widely you become known as a positive and outgoing person, the more likely you will be included in additional projects and opportunities to widen your network. You never know who might get promoted or leave the organization to join an employer on your target list!

Lastly, keep in mind that each time you connect with someone, you will very likely pick up some useful piece of information that will help you advance toward your goals. I have found this to be true when networking—you just need to be mindful about paying attention and gathering as much information as you can. All of this will pay off in the long term, and you might even have some immediate wins!

SUCCESS TIP 4: BALANCING FOR SUCCESS

You've probably heard people talking about the importance of work-life balance. This is very important to some people, while others prefer to put most of their time and energy into their professional lives. Neither approach is better than the other, in my opinion. You just need to identify which you prefer and live your life accordingly. It's mindfully being aware of how you want to balance your personal and professional lives that matters. And keep in mind that your balancing preference can change as you progress through your career.

Balancing Point: Motherhood

As women, we need to consider whether motherhood is in our future and, if so, how we will accommodate that important life stage into our Success Plan. If the question of motherhood is far away somewhere in the future for you, it's OK not to know how you want to approach it right now. But you should keep in mind that becoming a parent will very likely change your approach to work, at least for a period of several years. And, if and when that time comes, you may need to alter your Success Plan to some degree.

> **Personal Story: My Experience with Balancing Motherhood and Career**

In my twenties, I was pretty sure I didn't want to have children. I found the idea of having the freedom to do what I wanted without having the responsibility of a child attractive, and I had heard from others how expensive it can be to raise children. However, by my early thirties, those concerns had subsided and my personal life had changed quite a bit. I was married and had a stepson, and our daughter was born.

Over the course of the next few years, a lot changed for me. My focus shifted to being a mom rather than growing my career. Keep in mind that I did not have a Success Plan to guide me at the time. I was basically drifting along and enjoying motherhood. My career became more like a job—albeit a job I enjoyed—and thankfully led me back to my career eventually, but it was definitely less important than it had been in the past.

I turned my attention to helping our daughter explore activities like ballet, gymnastics, horseback riding, a range of sports, and even the violin. I became the leader of her Girl Scout troop, which took a lot of time and energy, but it was very rewarding. It was as though all the energy I used to pour into my professional life shifted almost entirely into being a mom. And I wouldn't trade a moment of it! I'm very proud of the way I shifted into motherhood.

However, I now know that if I had a Success Plan back then, I would have had the discipline and framework to mind my career a little more intentionally and perhaps not have lost as much professional momentum during that period. I don't regret focusing on bring a mom, I just think I could have gotten farther, faster, if I had a plan in place for my career during that period of my life.

Along the way, as my focus eventually shifted slightly back to my career, I decided to obtain an MBA so I could move into roles that required an advanced degree, as I mentioned earlier in this section. After I earned my degree, I was able to make a significant career move that required moving our family to another state. Our daughter was 13 at the time, definitely not an ideal age to be uprooted and moved away from family and friends. Mommy guilt followed, to be sure!

By this time, I had definitely shifted a lot of focus back on my career. It was difficult balancing my new, much more demanding role with being a wife and mother. I was fortunate to have a husband who supported my career aspirations. Our daughter eventually realized that moving wasn't really all that terrible and she made some wonderful, lifelong friends.

All of this happened without a plan, without a real sense of what I ultimately wanted to achieve with my career. I often wonder what might have materialized for me professionally if I had taken the time to create a Success Plan. Again, I have no regrets. I just would have advanced farther in less time if I had a well-thought-out plan that I was following.

If you believe strongly that you want to have children but do not want motherhood to lessen your focus on your career, be sure to look for a partner who doesn't mind assuming most of the parental duties. Thinking about this and planning for how you want to approach motherhood prior to having children can make a big difference in selecting your ideal partner and your overall happiness in life. I was very fortunate to find such a partner without being intentional about it. Don't depend on luck if you can avoid it, however!

When thinking about balancing, it's important to understand that you cannot perform every aspect of your life at 100 percent all the time. You must intentionally choose to focus on what matters most at present, and in accordance with your Success Plan. There are other life changes in addition to the potential of motherhood than can shift your focus throughout your life: finding a partner and adjusting to life together; moving for your partner's career and having to find a new job in a location that wasn't a part of your Success Plan; illness—your own or that of a loved one; caring for aging parents.

Many things can distract you from your professional life, and some of them can be life-enhancing. By having a Success Plan in place, however, you will more effectively navigate these distractions and remain as focused as possible on your career.

SUCCESS TIP 5: SHIFTING FOR SUCCESS

It's important to understand the concept of "shifting," which means changing your focus roughly each decade of your career as you gain more experience—from learning to managing, then leading, and ultimately to mentoring. In order to do this, imagine yourself at a 30,000-foot viewpoint rather than at ground level, out of the day-to-day details, as though you were sort of hovering over your career looking at your Success Plan as a whole. This can also be referred to as "getting out of the weeds" and thinking about your career in a larger context, including where you are now through the next 10 years and even to your retirement.

Based on my experience and observations of others over the years, this shifting process looks roughly as follows:

Learning

During the early stage of your career, which is typically in your 20s, you are in the "soak it up" period. Initially, you are learning what it's like to be in the workforce full time and how to navigate the work environment. You are also learning a lot about yourself and your selected career field, and might even decide you want to change to another industry.

During this phase, your emphasis must be on asking questions and learning as much as you can. Expectations from your leaders will be relatively low, initially. By that, I mean you aren't expected to know everything from day one. Take advantage of this time and learn. Make yourself more valuable by asking to help support special projects. Get exposed to as much as you can, gradually. Toward the end of this period, you will take on more responsibility and begin shifting into management opportunities.

Managing

Sometime during this period—which could occur during your late 20s or early 30s—you may shift into more of a management role. This could mean actually overseeing a team, or it could mean managing projects on your own. A lot of this depends on your workplace and the kinds of opportunities that exist. The main point here is that you begin to take on more responsibility and expectations increase.

This is an exciting time because you are at the point where you are putting everything you experienced during the learning phase to work and are feeling a greater sense of responsibility and fulfillment. You have likely reached your 3-year goals and have begun working toward your 5-year goals. Along the way, you have probably made adjustments to your Success Plan and goals, and you have used your marketing plan to help distinguish yourself as a rising star in your organization.

Leading

You will shift into a leadership role during this period, which typically takes place in your late 30s to early 40s. Now you have a much greater sense of responsibility and you have mastered a range of skills within your profession. You have probably completed your original Success Plan and have created a new one for the next 10 years of your career.

This period is fulfilling because you are seen as a leader in your organization and you are benefiting from the experience you gained through the learning and managing phases. Of course, you continue to learn and gain more experience during this phase. However, your focus has now shifted to leading others—both those on your team and individuals throughout the organization.

Mentoring

During this phase, which is usually during your 50s and beyond, you remain a leader and are likely at the top of your field. There may be another step or two in your career path, but everything you have experienced throughout your career is now coming together and you have achieved many of your goals. Your Success Plan probably focuses on retirement—when and how that will happen. And you find that you have both the time and interest to focus on helping others, although you have likely done this to some degree as you've moved through your career.

This is a rewarding phase. You are accomplished and able to spend dedicated time helping others succeed. While you remain very active in your career, your network may be changing to include more and more people that are looking to you for advice and guidance.

Insights: Gina's Thoughts on Shifting

Gina's career includes serving as Chief Operating Officer, Chief Marketing Officer, and ultimately Chairman of a large organization in the financial industry. She has since opened a consulting firm and counsels companies and their leaders on complex strategic issues and growth initiatives. I had the privilege of working with her when she was a board member of a former employer, and I always appreciated her insights and support.

I asked Gina to share some thoughts about the concept of shifting. Following are excerpts from her response.

"Over the course of your career, your priorities evolve. As a young professional, it is about learning, gaining credibility and responsibility, building relationships, and getting to know yourself. As you progress, it is more about expanding your role, driving results, and ascending to greater levels of responsibility and opportunity.

"At some point, you start to be driven more by personal satisfaction, developing talent, and helping others achieve their goals. You no longer feel like you have to 'prove yourself' every day and can really focus on making sure others are thriving and getting the visibility they need. Mentoring others becomes a priority. Your relationships, cultivated over many years, become invaluable to you and others. Be careful not to abuse them.

"In order to be effective at this level, you must have earned credibility in prior phases of your career and you must stay engaged/relevant. This is not a time of rest or complacency. You are still striving and driving results, but often in a different way.

"This phase is also an opportunity to continue learning and feeding your intellectual curiosity. Engaging with a different, often younger, group of people is a tremendous opportunity to broaden your knowledge and stay current on technology, trends, etc.

Embrace where you are and find ways to add value to yourself, your business, your community, and the people around you."

It's important to realize where you are in your career. Take advantage of this awareness so you avoid getting frustrated, trying to do too much too soon. If you are in the learning phase, take time to soak up as much as you can. If you are close to shifting into the managing phase, make sure your path will lead to taking on more responsibility. As you move into the leading phase, make sure you have prepared yourself for the increased expectations and accountability that it brings.

Keep in mind that these shifts can occur on a different schedule. Everyone's experience is unique, depending on the opportunities that exist. As discussed earlier in this section, motherhood will likely play an important role in when these shifts occur for you. Let yourself move into the phases on your own schedule and remain aware of how this is working for you. Take time every year or so to go to that 30,000-foot viewpoint and have a look around. Make changes to your Success Plan if needed. This is an ongoing process of managing your career to your best advantage, based on where you are in life. Be sure to avoid simply drifting along!

Insights: Professional Guidance from Kathleen

Remember Kathleen from the end of Section One? As I explained, her focus on relationships really sets her apart. She has been very supportive of me through the process of writing this book—to the point of actually wanting to get involved and offer some Success Tips of her own! As you read them, picture in your mind an amazing woman who owns a digital marketing firm, is very involved in client relationships, is married to a man who has his own business as well, and has a young son. Taking the time to share her thoughts with you, in between everything else she is balancing, really says a lot about her.

"Most of the success I've found as a business owner stems from an ability to learn and adapt.

"At the beginning of my career, I accepted a marketing position at a start-up automotive digital agency without any formal education in advertising, a field that is always evolving. This is where my ability to learn on the job became critical.

"During my first week on the job, I emailed my boss a question about an event I was assigned. He sent me a 'Let Me Google That for You' link, demonstrating how I could easily have found that information on my own. That was the last time I ever asked a question without first doing some research!

"During these formative years of my career, the following three tips helped me stay ahead of the game:

1. ***Keep a question section during meetings.*** *In your notes, reserve a section where you can jot down unknown acronyms and any questions you have. This way, you can look into it later without disrupting the meeting.*

2. ***Do your research prior to asking questions.*** *If you're unable to find an answer, ask the right person your question and share what you've learned via your own research. If applicable, present a potential solution to the issue. This allows conversations with your mentors and leaders to go much deeper, expanding your knowledge exponentially while demonstrating your thought process and competencies as a problem solver.*

3. ***Sign up for industry-specific newsletters.*** *Set aside a few hours per month to take a deep dive into current trends and what experts are saying. This is related to Success Tip 2: Learning for Success.*

"I'm now over a decade into my career, and while I haven't stopped learning, I have shifted away from general job knowledge and soaking everything up. Now I'm learning how to help my team lead, continue our agency's growth, and expand our offerings through the development of new products or software."

I hope you have an opportunity to work with women like Gina and Kathleen during your career. They are truly inspirational and always motivate me to do more, take that extra step, and find more hours in the day!

In the next section, I will wrap up everything you have accomplished in creating your Success Plan and navigating through this book. Time for action!

WRAPPING IT ALL UP: GET READY TO SUCCEED!

••

Now it's time to get out there and begin fulfilling your Success Plan! Take a moment to review everything you have created:

- **Core Values**: Five values to help guide you in navigating your career

- **Optional Supporting Behaviors**: Additional guideposts to support living by your core values

- **Focus Statement**: A sentence or two that bring your core values to life

- **10-Year Goals**: Where you aspire to be in your career 10 years from today

- **5-Year Goals**: What you must accomplish by the halfway point

- **3-Year Goals with Milestones**: A set of foundational goals with tangible markers of success

- **Marketing Plan with Measures of Success**: A roadmap for positioning yourself for success

You have a plan for **continually visualizing** your 3-, 5-, and 10-year goals, with a specific cadence for each set. You know it is important to visualize your immediate goals on a daily basis, your mid-range goals monthly or every other month, and your long-range goals less frequently, but at least quarterly. You know that by visualizing your goals without being concerned about the specifics of how you will achieve them, **"the how" will come to you at the right time along the way**.

In addition, you have been armed with a number of **Success Tips** to support you in achieving your goals and positioning yourself as a rising star in your chosen profession. You now know how to:

- **Attract success** by leveraging the **Law of Attraction**, being **grateful and positive**, and **creating the culture (or micro-culture) you want** in the workplace.

- **Continually learn and invest in yourself**, including the decision regarding whether to obtain an advanced degree, if applicable.

- **Develop your professional network**, along with a plan for how you will remain in contact with each of your categorized contacts.

- **Balance your life according to your preferences** and plan ahead regarding whether motherhood will be a part of your life—and if so, how you will accommodate it into your Success Plan.

- **Understand, appreciate, and take advantage of where you are in the shifting stages of your career**—learning, managing, leading, or mentoring.

Think about where you were when you started the process of creating your Success Plan and contrast that with where you are right now. Recall any struggles you encountered along the way and be grateful for how you worked through them. Reflect on what you learned about yourself through this process. Were there any aha moments? Did anything new come up when developing your goals or positioning objectives that you hadn't really considered in the past?

Realize that you are now ready to embark on an amazing journey over the next 10 years and beyond! As you achieve your 3- and 5-year goals, begin extending your Success Plan past the 10-year mark. Maybe you add another 5 years to your plan, or perhaps you go for an additional 10 years. Know that your Success Plan will continually evolve as you do, and it will very likely change along the way. You have given yourself permission to make these revisions as needed. Changes to your plan do not signify failure, but rather growth and continual advancement.

One last assignment: join the Success Plan community, if you haven't already, and keep in touch. Take advantage of the discounted membership rate you receive because you purchased this book at http://www.creatingyoursuccessplan.com/community-offer. Reach out to community members to share your struggles and to offer support. Let me know how you are progressing with your Success Plan and how I might provide guidance. As women, we are all in this together and we truly can bring my intention for you to fruition—to move forward in a positive, proactive manner to a very rewarding professional life. As more of us do this, I believe the gender disparities in leadership roles will narrow and eventually dissolve. It's an exciting time to be a woman in the workforce!

Here's to your success, always!

ACKNOWLEDGMENTS

Writing this book has been very fulfilling and personally rewarding. Along the way, I received tremendous support from many people who shared insights and encouragement.

Big shout-out to my "focus group," which included Hailey, Rachel, Grace, Lexi, Ashley, London, Sarah (see more below), and Chloe—each of them fall into the category of women for whom this book is written. Their professional experience ranges from the early- to mid-career stages, and they have been a source of inspiration for me. Their insights and encouragement were invaluable as I moved forward with this work.

I'd like to further recognize Sarah for creating the Success Plan infographic and helping me finesse the book cover design. She is a very talented designer who doesn't usually freelance but made an exception for me because she believes in this work.

A special thanks to the women who provided insights and allowed me to help bring parts of the book to life by sharing stories and guidance from their professional experience. You read about my daughter Blaire's experience learning about the power of positivity, Angie's exceptional ability to create a positive micro-culture, Jessica's smart use of networking to navigate a career transition, and Gina's insights into how we shift into different stages throughout our careers. In addition, you read Kathleen's insights on the Success Plan components, and she shared some of her own Success Tips in section two. Each of these women have impacted my life in ways that I will always be grateful for, and I am thrilled to be able to introduce them to you through this book.

Of course, I must acknowledge my husband, Ed. He has been a source of love, support, and balance in my life for more than 30 years. Throughout the process of writing this book, he provided encouragement, peeking into the study each morning as I was typing away, offering a smile and a cup of tea occasionally, and mainly just trying not to interrupt. And he's always proud of me, no matter what I get myself into!

And one last thanks to Blaire. After I told her I was going to write this book, she told a friend that she had just found out her mother was a "bad ass." What a fabulous compliment!

ABOUT THE AUTHOR

Janice Lamy is an accomplished marketing professional with more than thirty years of experience leading successful marketing programs and mentoring young professionals. She brings in-depth expertise in creating programs and processes aimed at fueling exceptional productivity and generating fresh revenue. A creative problem solver, instructor, team leader and communicator, Janice has a proven ability to develop marketing and communications strategies designed to increase efficiency while substantially heightening performance levels.

Throughout her career, Janice has enjoyed serving as a mentor to others and offering guidance based upon her experience and observations. She finds fulfillment in watching young professionals grow into their careers and achieve their goals and aspirations. She is keenly interested in positively impacting a generation of women by providing career success guidance through her book and online resources. She sees a convergence of activity from many sources coming together to address the disparities between women and men in leadership roles. By helping women create their Success Plans, her intention is to contribute to that movement in a meaningful way.

www.ingramcontent.com/pod-product-compliance
Lightning Source LLC
Chambersburg PA
CBHW030223170426
43194CB00007BA/837